When Gerda Weissmann Klein wrote *The Blue Rose*— the story of Jenny—over 30 years ago, she hoped that the book would help readers accept and love unconditionally every child who was physically or mentally challenged. After its publication in 1974 and its inclusion in the *Reader's Digest*, thousands of letters were received from around the world—many from families with blue roses, many from caregivers, and many from people with concern and compassion. That same year, The Blue Rose Foundation was created by Peggy Cohen, Lillian Gerstman, and Berna Koren as a vehicle to promote respect and understanding for those with developmental disabilities such as Jenny's and to advance their well-being. For decades, the Foundation has contributed funds to help initiatives such as a group home, a greenhouse, and numerous special projects.

In the 1970s, thousands of parents, including Jenny's mother, joined educators and other professionals to push for legislation to protect the rights of those with disabilities and to ensure needed services. Although much has been accomplished, more needs to be done. Today, a new wave of advocates is focused on the mysterious surge of autism spectrum disorders, and as before, there is a need for organizations like The Blue Rose Foundation.

Requests for *The Blue Rose* book have continued, and it became apparent that an updated edition of the book for a new generation should be published. Gerda Klein and The Blue Rose Foundation joined together to make it happen. Thanks to the cooperation of Hoover Elementary School in Kenmore, New York, a beautiful new face – Kelsie Skinner – represents Jenny. Kelsie and her brother, Mitchell, as well as Hoover students, teachers and staff are featured, along with a tailless cat named Goose. The heartwarming new photographic images and book design are a tribute to the professionalism and sensitivity of photographer Errol Daniels and designer Ben Richey, respectively.

Jeff Sapp and Kate Esposito developed a wonderful teacher's lesson plan to accompany the book. Mary Ann Lauricella and Dr. Pamela Johnson contributed much to adapting the original narrative for contemporary readers. Many individuals, groups and agencies—too numerous to mention— have graciously participated in the preparation of this new edition.

To those named and those unnamed, we owe our thanks. They have made it possible for *The Blue Rose* to grow and blossom again.

A Mother's Foreword

My daughter Jenny was the original "blue rose." She was six years old in 1968, attending a class for educable retarded children when our friend and neighbor, Gerda Weissmann Klein, wrote the first edition of *The Blue Rose*. When the book was finally published, Jenny was twelve years old, attending a special residential school.

Now Jenny is forty-five, living with other developmentally challenged adults on the grounds of a former state institution, waiting for a group home in Western New York. As a child, she was not included in the educational and social life of her cohort or her community. She was truly an isolated blue rose.

In this revised edition of *The Blue Rose*, we meet a new Jenny who has been blessed with the benefits of legislation, both federal and state. Included in the world of her peers throughout her life, our new young Jenny—unlike the blue roses of Jenny's generation—has been given opportunities and tools to more fully reach her potential as a human being.

Thousands of parents, professionals, legislators, and community activists are responsible for expanding the horizons of all of our blue roses. Also, for over three decades, the members of The Blue Rose Foundation have worked ceaselessly to promote community education and raise money for innovative, inclusive programs and projects.

On behalf of all our blue roses, I want to extend a special thank you to Gerda Weissmann Klein, whose sensitivity and talent help mobilize both old and new generations.

Lillian Innerfield Gerstman
Jenny's mother

Jenny Innerfield first inspired this book on her sixth birthday, the fourth of July, over forty years ago. In 2008, Jenny's life continues to inspire me. I dedicate this book to her, once again, with gratitude for all she has taught me and with my abiding love.

GWK

Jenny is a young girl—a child we love.
She has brown eyes and dark brown hair.

If her hair falls into her eyes
she brushes it away, but her hand does
not go straight to her forehead.

Instead it curves around like
a flower first opening its petals.
Then she brushes her hair out of her eyes.

She looks up at you and smiles.
Her nose wrinkles, her lips curve up at the corners,
she says, "Hi.—Hi Jenny."
She repeats, "Hi, hi, hi."

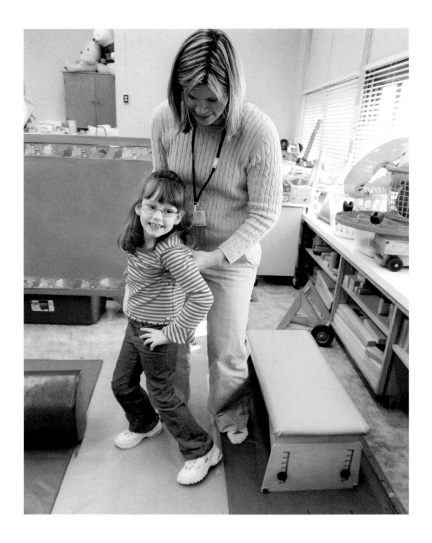

Sometimes she goes into an awkward little dance.

You see, Jenny is different.
Different?
Yes, different from most other children.
But surely all people don't have to be alike,
think alike,
act alike
or look alike.

To me, Jenny is like a blue rose.

A *blue* rose?

Have you ever seen a blue rose?
There are white roses
and pink roses
and yellow roses,
and of course lots of red roses.
But blue?

Every gardener would love to raise a blue rose.
People would come from near and far to see it.
It is different and beautiful.
Jenny is different, too,
and so, in a way,
she is like a blue rose.

This is the story of Jenny.
We know her well. She is our friend.
Jenny was born on the 4th of July.

What fun!

She likes to be told over and over
about the day she was born.
It was a summer day,
not a cloud in the blue sky.
A day warm and golden with sunshine.

Jenny's family was at the hospital,
and Jenny's older brother went with us.
What a lucky person Jenny is, we often say,
to be born on the 4th of July.

Her birthday will always be a national holiday.

We often talked of the years ahead.
Jenny growing up,
learning to walk,
to talk.
Jenny going to school,

Jenny on a day far, far away
being a grownup young adult . . .
and having a place of her own.

Jenny's family and our children were very excited by the idea
that they would be able to say,
"We remember the day when Jenny was born."

And then Jenny came home from the hospital.
A pink baby, all cuddly and round.
At the beginning Jenny cried very often.
She cried more than most babies.

Why?

Well, perhaps
she saw different shadows that frightened her.
Perhaps she heard sounds that were strange to her.
When she was older,
Jenny always stayed close to her mother and held on to her tightly.

You know, when a kitten loses its tail,
it is said to gain sharper ears.
It's true that a tail helps a kitten run faster.
But a kitten without a tail hears better
and can detect approaching footsteps
long before other kittens do.

Some people don't know about such a kitten's fine ears;
they only see the lack of a tail.

Some children are mean and cruel and stare:
the kitten has no tail,
the kitten has no tail!
Sometimes Jenny would run up to her mother and clutch her tightly.
For no apparent reason at all.
At least, for none that we could see.

Jenny often worried.

And so we came to understand
that Jenny's world was a little different,
unknown to us, in some ways.

We began to think that she was in a world
in which *we* might not feel completely at home.
To go there might, in a way,
be like going to another planet.

What if we were astronauts
who landed on a distant planet?
How carefully we would step onto the surface,
slowly testing the ground we didn't know.

People who already live there would watch us;
they might not understand
our fears of their world.
Because it is their world,
they feel at home in it and know it well.

We would be heroes to people on our earth;
they would marvel at what we accomplished.

But to the people on the new planet,
we might look quite different.

They might call us slow, strange,
in a world of our own.

So, too, maybe Jenny sees things
with different eyes.
Maybe, also, she hears a different drummer.
In a way, it's as if Jenny is standing behind a screen,
a screen we cannot see.
Maybe it has beautiful colors such as we never see.
Maybe the colors distract Jenny at times
from paying attention when we talk to her.
Perhaps she listens to music we cannot hear.
It is said that fish have a language
and a music of their own—
a language and music, carried by the waves.
Music *we* cannot hear because
our ears are not fine enough.

So Jenny might hear sounds we never hear.
Maybe that is why she jumps up at times
and goes into her awkward dance.

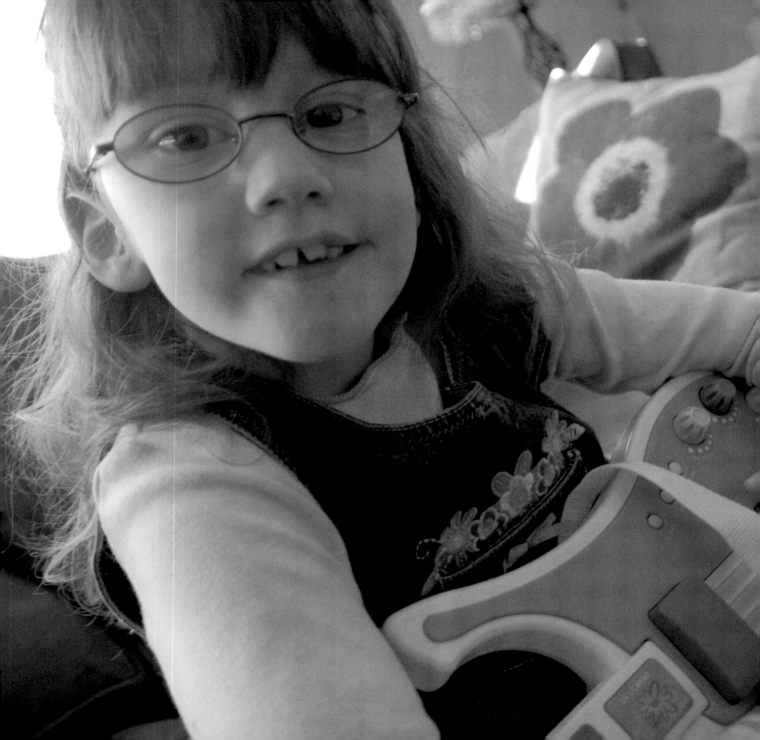

I sometimes think Jenny is like a bird,
a bird with very short wings.
For such a bird, flying is very hard:
it takes more strength, more effort, more time.
A bird with ordinary wings takes flying for granted,
but the bird with short wings
has to work much harder at learning,
and in a way, it has to be smarter.

For Jenny to learn things to say and to read
or even to hop and skip, is very difficult.

And so, therefore,
we have to understand
how much she has accomplished
when she does learn something.

But there is another Jenny.
A Jenny who on a stormy
winter afternoon
sits in her rocking chair alone
and rocks,
holding her doll in her arms.
She is very troubled
and puzzled.

And her eyes tell a story—
a story filled with pain.
"Jack says I'm weird, retarded.
What does that mean, Mommy?
Weird, retarded.
The children say things and laugh.

Why?"

And Jenny rocks in her chair and her eyes look like stars in the twilight.

There are many things Jenny does not understand.

And there are many things other people don't understand about
Jenny—that Jenny is like a kitten without a tail,
that Jenny hears different music, that she is like a bird with shorter wings
and has her own ways to fly.

Jenny is like a blue rose, remarkable and memorable. And because
blue roses are so mysterious, we don't know much about them.